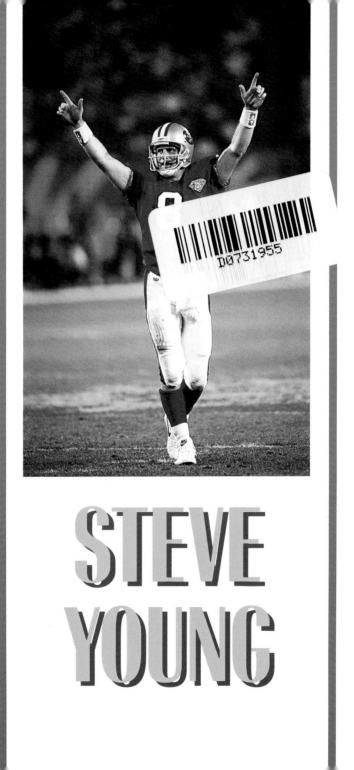

STEVE
YOUNG

THE ACHIEVERS

STEVE YOUNG

COMPLETE QUARTERBACK

Terri Morgan and Shmuel Thaler

 Lerner Publications Company ● Minneapolis

For my friends Tom and Laura Crosser
—Terri Morgan
For my daughter Kayla and niece Jordan,
the next generation
—Shmuel Thaler

Information for this book was obtained from the
following sources:
Boy's Life, Brigham Young University Sports Information Office,
*Building a Champion: On Football and the Making of the
49ers* by Bill Walsh with Glen Dickey, *Church News, Deseret
News*, interviews with Steve's high school math teacher Terry
Lowe, *Rocky Mountain News, San Francisco Chronicle, San
Jose Mercury News, Sport, Sports Illustrated, The Sporting
News, Total Impact* by Ronnie Lott with Jill Leiber.

This book is available in two editions:
Library binding by Lerner Publications Company
Soft cover by First Avenue Editions
241 First Avenue North, Minneapolis, Minnesota 55401

International Standard Book Number: 0-8225-2886-X (lib. bdg.)
International Standard Book Number: 0-8225-9716-0 (pbk.)

LIBRARY OF CONGRESS CATALOGING-IN-PUBLICATION DATA

Morgan, Terri.
    Steve Young : complete quarterback / Terri Morgan and Shmuel Thaler.
        p.   cm. — (The Achievers)
    Includes bibliographical references.
    ISBN 0-8225-2886-X (alk. paper)
    ISBN 0-8225-9716-0 (pbk. : alk. paper)
    1. Young, Steve, 1961–   — Juvenile literature. 2. Football players —
United States — Biography — Juvenile literature. 3. San Francisco
49ers (Football team) — Juvenile literature. I. Thaler, Shmuel. II. Title.
III. Series.
GV939.Y69M67   1996
796.332'092—dc20
[B]   95–20179

Manufactured in the United States of America
2 3 4 5 6 7 – JR – 01 00 99 98 97 96

Contents

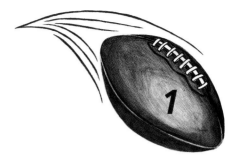

Proving Himself

It was the day before Super Bowl XXIX (29), and San Francisco 49er Steve Young could hardly wait. For 25 of his 33 years, the lefthanded quarterback had dreamed about leading a team to victory in football's biggest game. Now he was in Miami, just 24 hours away from the biggest sporting challenge of his life. It was a game he had been preparing for ever since he first put on pads and a helmet as an eight-year-old playing in a pee wee league.

Steve had been to the Super Bowl twice before— in 1989 and 1990. He had watched from the sidelines as quarterback Joe Montana led the 49ers to back-to-back Super Bowl victories. Now in January 1995, it was his turn to guide the San Francisco offense with the world championship on the line. After 10 seasons in the National Football League (NFL), including 4 as Montana's backup, Young was eager to prove himself.

A Super Bowl victory was the only thing missing in Steve's long and exciting football career. Despite dozens of outstanding games, three consecutive NFL passing titles, two trips to the Pro Bowl, and NFL most valuable player awards in 1992 and 1994, some fans and reporters were still critical of Steve. Angry that he had replaced Montana as the 49ers quarterback, disgruntled fans complained that Steve had never won the *big* game.

San Francisco defeated its archrival, the Dallas Cowboys, 38-28 in the National Football Conference (NFC) Championship Game and hushed most, but not all, of those critics. Steve would have to win the Super Bowl to prove he was worthy of replacing Montana.

The 49ers were heavily favored to defeat the American Football Conference (AFC) San Diego Chargers in Super Bowl XXIX. Steve knew San Francisco should win if the team, which had beaten the Chargers in both the preseason and the regular season, played up to its potential. If the underdogs from San Diego upset San Francisco for any reason, many fans would blame Steve for the loss. "If he failed to win," said Steve's mother, Sherry, "the fans in San Francisco would have tarred and feathered him."

The anticipation was overwhelming. Steve knew he had to burn off some of his nervous excitement.

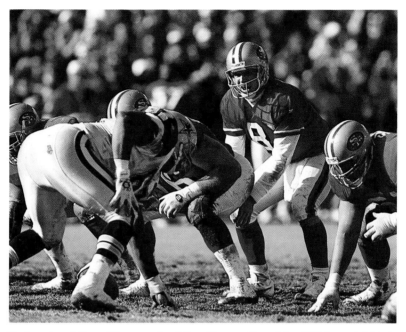
Dallas kept the 49ers out of the Super Bowl in 1993 and 1994.

With no more practices scheduled and swarms of fans and reporters waiting outside, Steve was stuck in the team hotel.

Normally when the 49ers play away from home, players share hotel rooms. As a reward for getting to the Super Bowl, the 49ers owners had arranged for private suites for Steve and the eight other star players who had been invited to play in the postseason Pro Bowl game. Alone in his suite, Steve grew even more anxious. To keep from worrying about the upcoming game, he decided to follow his normal pregame routine. He and tight end Brent Jones, who normally roomed together, carried the bed from Steve's room into Jones' suite. Then the two players settled in for the evening to talk about football and watch movies.

Their conversation covered everything but the Super Bowl, Jones said later. Steve, an avid movie fan, watched *The Shadow* before going to sleep. The next morning, he and Jones killed time by watching the movie again. About six hours before kickoff, they couldn't wait any longer. The two called for a cab and headed for Miami's Joe Robbie Stadium.

In the locker room, Steve's teammates took turns distracting him with conversation. Finally, it was time to suit up. Just before running onto the field for the pregame introductions, tackle Harris Barton ran his hands down the back of Steve's jersey. The action, a regular pregame ritual for the two, was meant to wipe the invisible monkey off Steve's back. "This is the last time I'm going to have to do this," Barton told Steve.

Just 1 minute and 24 seconds into the game, Barton realized how true his words were. The 49ers won the coin toss, and chose to receive the ball. Steve threw to John Taylor for an 11-yard gain. Then the 49ers rushed for 7 yards. On his third play of the game, Steve threw the ball to Jerry Rice, who caught it in the end zone for the 49ers' first touchdown.

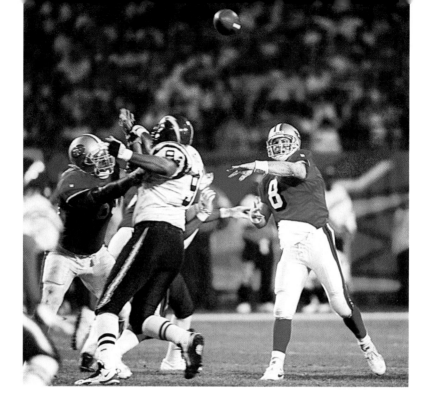

On San Francisco's next possession, less than two minutes later, Steve scrambled 21 yards for a first down. Then he threw a 51-yard pass to Ricky Watters for another 49er touchdown. The Niners had moved the ball 79 yards in four plays for their second score.

San Diego got on the scoreboard late in the first quarter, but never really threatened the Niners. Steve passed for two more touchdowns in the second quarter. The Chargers scored only a field goal.

Steve led San Francisco to two more touchdowns in the third quarter. The 49ers also scored on a run. Steve set a Super Bowl record in the fourth quarter

Steve threw six TD passes in the 1995 Super Bowl.

when he threw his sixth touchdown pass. The old record of five touchdown passes was set by Joe Montana, interestingly enough, in a 1990 game against Denver. The 7-yard completion to Rice gave the 49ers a 49-18 lead. Rice, who hauled in 10 passes for 149 yards and 3 touchdowns, was the 49ers' top receiver.

In the final period, after San Francisco head coach George Seifert had taken most of his starters out of the game, the Chargers scored another touchdown. When the clock ran out, San Francisco had defeated the Chargers, 49-26. Steve finally had the Super Bowl title he'd been wanting for so long. The ecstatic quarterback ran a victory lap around the field while San Francisco fans chanted his name.

"Whatever critics he may have had, Steve Young proved tonight that he's one of the greatest quarterbacks of all time," Coach Seifert said after the game. Steve had completed 24 of the 36 passes he had attempted for 325 yards. Steve had also rushed for 49 yards. San Diego's defenders hadn't intercepted a single pass. Steve was named the Most Valuable Player of the Super Bowl for his outstanding performance.

"It was a great game," Young said. "We had to fight through some difficult times (during the season) and we were able to move ahead and play some great football, maybe some of the best football that's ever been played. We're proud of that."

Steve once pitched a no-hitter in high school.

14

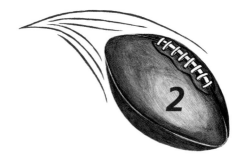

Growing Up with Grit

Jon Steven Young was born on October 11, 1961, in Salt Lake City, Utah. Steve is the oldest of Sherry and LeGrande Young's five children. Steve's father had been the starting halfback for Brigham Young University in the 1950s. Although his name is LeGrande, his relatives and friends call him Grit. His college teammates gave him that nickname because of his determination on the football field. After college, he became a lawyer. Steve's mother, who also attended BYU, taught Sunday school classes and took care of the family. His brother Mike was born when Steve was two, and his sister Melissa arrived when he was four. Tom was born in 1969, when Steve was eight. Steve's youngest brother, Jim, is 17 years younger than Steve.

Steve's great-great-great-grandfather, Brigham Young, was an early leader in the Mormon church.

Brigham Young was a powerful figure in Utah's early days.

The Mormon church is called the Church of Jesus Christ of Latter-day Saints. Brigham Young also helped start the university in Utah that carries his name. Born in 1801, Brigham Young took over as president of the Mormon church in 1847 when founder Joseph Smith died. Young led the migration of Mormons into Utah, and oversaw construction of Salt Lake City. From 1850, when Utah was made a United States territory, until 1857, Young was governor. "It's fun and interesting," Steve said of his famous ancestor, "but it doesn't get me anywhere."

As a youngster, Steve loved sports, just like the rest of his family. Even as a toddler, Steve was athletic. "He was particularly coordinated," his father recalled. "I was doing push-ups once and Steve came along and asked if he could do them. He was only two and a half. I said sure, and he did 10 of them."

By age three, Steve could dribble a basketball. He had so much energy and enthusiasm that he bounced on his toes when he walked. His family called him Springy because he was always springing around the house.

When Steve was six, the family moved to the East Coast. The Youngs first settled in Scarsdale, New York. A few years later, they moved 15 miles away, to a modest, two-story home on Split Timber Road in Greenwich, Connecticut.

In Greenwich, the family's leisure time revolved around athletic events. The children loved playing sports, and Sherry and Grit encouraged them to compete. The boys played football, basketball, and baseball. Melissa excelled as a swimmer. Whenever any of the children had a game or a meet scheduled, they knew that at least one parent would be there to watch. When the children's competitions overlapped, Sherry would attend one game while Grit went to another.

The Mormon religion was also important to the Young family. Six days a week, Monday through Saturday, the Youngs would get up at 5 A.M. to go to church services before school and work. There weren't very many other Mormon families in Greenwich when Steve was growing up. The Youngs had to drive 30 miles to the nearest church.

"Mormonism is a lifestyle, more than just a Sunday thing," Steve said. Like most practicing Mormons, the Youngs lived by a strict ethical code. They tithed, which means they donated 10 percent of their income to the church. They also didn't drink alcohol, coffee, or caffeinated soda pop. They didn't smoke cigarettes or swear.

At first, Steve followed the Mormon rules because his parents wanted him to behave that way. By the time he was a teenager, however, he had chosen Mormonism for his own way of life.

Grit was a strict but loving father. He set high standards for his five children.

"If I told my father I was going out at night," Steve said, "he'd want to know what time I was coming home. If I was one minute late, he'd be at the doorstep waiting for me."

Steve (No. 14) was a quarterback in high school.

There was no room for compromise with Grit. "When Mr. Young told you to do something, you didn't question it," said Frank Arnone, who grew up in the neighborhood. He compared Steve's dad to the television father of the *Leave it to Beaver* show. "He was like Mr. Cleaver on steroids."

The biggest rule in the Young household, Steve recalls, was that you didn't break any of Dad's rules. "He didn't like it if you didn't live up to your end of a bargain," Steve said. "He never hit any of us. He didn't have to. He'd give you that look, the one where you'd just disappointed him."

As he was growing up, Steve looked up to his father and hated to disappoint him. "I truly respect him," Steve said. "I can't tell you how grateful I am for the way I was raised. As tough as my father was, he was always fair."

Steve also admires his father's strong work ethic. Grit believes in working hard. He encouraged his children to have after-school and summer jobs so they, too, could learn the value of hard work. When Steve wasn't in school, at church, or playing sports, he was mowing lawns, delivering newspapers, or scooping ice cream at a local store. "If I didn't have a job, I couldn't use the car," Steve recalls. "I was always working, so he'd let me borrow the car."

Although Grit was a successful attorney, the family maintained a low-key, down-to-earth lifestyle. Sherry and Grit wanted to teach their children the value of money. When the family car broke down, Grit would raise the hood and repair it himself. For years he told his children he made just six dollars a day. "We believed him," Steve's sister, Melissa, said. "We thought we were the poorest people in the world."

Steve's strict upbringing and religious beliefs didn't stop him from having fun. At Greenwich High School, Steve was a popular and well-respected student. "He was one of those rare kids with a wonderful ability to cross every clique in school," said Terry Lowe, Steve's calculus teacher in his junior and senior years.

Throughout high school, Steve dated Christy Fichtner, who later won the Miss USA pageant. Steve often went out with his friends in the evenings as well. "I was the guy who drove everyone else home," he said. "They'd buy their beer and they'd buy me a gallon of milk and we'd have chugging contests. I look back on high school and I can't imagine anyone having more fun than I did."

Steve lettered in football, basketball, and baseball at Greenwich High School. As a sophomore, though, he had some rough moments on the football field. During one junior varsity game that he started at quarterback, Steve's opponents intercepted him eight times. "As you can guess, we lost," he said of the game, which he still says is the worst of his career.

Steve's high school friend, Christy Fichtner, was crowned Miss USA in 1986.

On the varsity team, Steve rarely was intercepted, mainly because the Greenwich Cardinals played a wishbone, run-oriented offense. "We passed maybe 10 times a game," Steve said. "I was embarrassed to throw in public. I didn't enjoy throwing, because I wasn't very good at it."

During his senior year in high school, Steve was captain of the football, basketball, and baseball teams. The day after his senior prom, Steve pitched a no-hitter.

An excellent student, Steve worked as hard on his academic skills as he did on his athletic skills. He thrived on challenges in the classroom and took advanced-placement courses to prepare himself for college. "One of the things I remember about him was how bright he was, how enthusiastic he was and how disciplined he was with a task at hand," said Steve's former math teacher, Terry Lowe. "Calculus was not easy for Steve, but he decided he was going to lick it. He faced the challenge, and went on to conquer it."

By the time he graduated with a 4.1 grade-point average, Steve was fluent in French, a member of the National Honor Society, and a National Merit Scholarship finalist. He also had taken time to do volunteer work with mentally retarded children and to be president of the youth group at his church.

24

Big Man at BYU

Steve's academic record, along with his athletic ability, interested many college recruiters. His speed also impressed coaches. The 6-foot, 1-inch, 198-pound senior could run 40 yards in a blazing 4.5 seconds. More than half a dozen colleges offered Steve a scholarship.

Steve liked North Carolina's football program because it emphasized the running game he had played in high school. Grit, however, advised his son to select a school that best suited his educational goals. A football career can end any time with a single hit, Grit reminded Steve. An education lasts a lifetime.

With that in mind, Steve decided to attend Brigham Young University. "When it came time to decide on a school, I threw out football," said Steve, who planned to study accounting and international relations. "Otherwise, BYU would have been my last choice."

The university gave Steve a full scholarship, but during his first year at the Provo, Utah, campus, Steve regretted his decision. He was 2,500 miles from home and missed his family. When Steve showed up for his first practice, he was the No. 8 quarterback on the depth chart. The BYU coaches thought seven other players would be better quarterbacks than Steve. The coaches didn't think Steve's arm was strong enough for him to play quarterback. They wanted him to switch positions and play wide receiver, running back, or defensive back.

Steve did little to change the coaches' minds on his first day. When he lined up with the other quarterbacks to do passing drills, Steve took his first snap, stepped back to pass, and tripped over his own feet. "Everyone laughed," he recalls. "I was so embarrassed."

Despite his rocky start, Steve knew he could play quarterback. He refused to switch positions and spent most of the 1980 season watching from the sidelines. "I was eighth string, which is like being in the choir and singing from another part of the church," Steve said.

Discouraged and homesick, he called his parents often. One day he told Grit he wanted to quit the team. "My father told me, 'You can quit, but you can't come home and live here because I don't live with quitters,'" Steve said. "I decided to stay."

Grit was more understanding when Steve complained that it was hard to get around Provo without a car. Grit drove the family car, a 1965 Oldsmobile, to Utah and gave it to his oldest son. "Then he gave me his usual lecture on how important the car had been to the family, and to take good care of it," Steve said. He nicknamed the 14-year-old vehicle The Cardinal, although he and his friends also called the big car the "Tuna Boat."

The car allowed Steve to visit friends, like Doug and Barbara Schaerrer and their four children. They invited the homesick freshman to their home to watch *Monday Night Football* and share their meals. "He'd be watching on the floor and half the time, he'd fall asleep," Barbara Schaerrer said. "We just loved him. He was so personable and appreciative. He'd bring four or five ballplayers with him, and they felt right at home."

At football practice, Steve spent most of his time studying the play of BYU's star quarterback, Jim McMahon. Steve watched every move McMahon made on the field. McMahon had record-breaking seasons for BYU in 1980 and 1981—Steve's freshman and sophomore years. McMahon was an excellent quarterback but a reluctant teacher. He wasn't interested in helping Steve and was impatient when the young quarterback asked questions. "I tried to pick up as much on my own as I could," Steve said.

Steve learned from quarterback Jim McMahon, left, and coach LaVell Edwards while he played for BYU.

Steve's standing on the team improved during spring practice in 1981. Ted Tollner, BYU's new offensive coach, was impressed when he saw Steve throw during drills. Tollner talked to head coach LaVell Edwards. When Edwards saw Steve's crisp and accurate passes, he began to move him up on the depth chart. By the end of the spring, Steve was BYU's No. 2 quarterback, behind Jim McMahon.

Steve didn't play much in the 1981 season until McMahon hurt his knee during the fourth game. Steve replaced him and passed for two touchdowns as the BYU Cougars overpowered Colorado, 41-20. "Steve has come along faster, and from a greater distance, than any of our quarterbacks," Coach Edwards said after the game.

The sophomore quarterback got his first start the following week, against Utah State University. Steve's first pass was intended for wide receiver Dan Plater, but he threw the ball about 10 feet above Plater's head and about 10 feet beyond him. "I was sort of leery and not confident at first," Steve said. "I was floating the ball." As the game progressed, Steve put more zip on his passes and found his receivers. He connected 21 times in 40 attempts for 307 yards. He passed for one of BYU's four touchdowns, and the Cougars extended their record to 5-0 with a 32-26 victory.

Steve played well in his second start, a 45-41 loss to the University of Nevada at Las Vegas. But McMahon returned to action the following week, and Steve went back to the sidelines. BYU finished the season 10-2, and won its sixth straight Western Athletic Conference (WAC) football championship.

Steve won BYU's starting quarterback slot in 1982. McMahon had set 70 National Collegiate Athletic Association (NCAA) records for passing and total offense while at Brigham Young University. Now he was playing for the Chicago Bears in the NFL. His departure gave Steve, then a junior, a chance to shine. A great rusher, Steve was one of the team's fastest players. He wasn't afraid to run the ball, although Coach Edwards cringed when opponents tackled his quarterback.

BYU won its seventh consecutive WAC title in 1982 with an 8-4 record. Steve rushed for 640 yards and 10 touchdowns. His passing record was even more impressive. He threw for 3,100 yards and 18 touchdowns and was the Western Athletic Conference Offensive Player of the Year for 1982.

A few months later, tragedy struck. Steve had gone home for vacation. In April, he and two friends, Jill Simmons and Eric Hunn, were driving back to school from Connecticut. Steve was at the wheel until they reached Nebraska. Then it was Jill's turn to drive. Ten minutes after she took the wheel, the car left the road and flipped six times. Jill, 19, died instantly. Eric and Steve weren't injured.

Jill's death helped Steve realize how important it is to live life to its fullest. "It brought a lot of things into focus," Steve said. "You find yourself not putting so much emphasis on things you did before. You find there's a lot more to life."

Steve tried to put his grief behind him when the 1983 football season started. Baylor University nipped the Cougars, 40-36, in BYU's opener. The Cougars, however, reeled off 11 consecutive victories en route to their eighth straight WAC title. Quarterback Steve Young and tight end Gordon Hudson led the squad, Coach Edwards told reporters. He'd coached some great teams, the coach added, but the 1983 team was his best.

Steve was the No. 1 college passer in the nation in 1983 and he led the NCAA in total offense. He averaged 395 yards per game, 120 yards more than the runner-up. In one game, a 55-7 victory over archrival Utah State, he threw for six touchdowns. Steve tied or set 13 NCAA records, was named to eight different All-America first teams, and was runner-up for the Heisman Trophy. He capped his collegiate career by leading BYU to a 21-17 victory over Missouri in the Holiday Bowl. Professional coaches and sportswriters were predicting that Steve Young—BYU's former No. 8 quarterback—would be the first player chosen in the 1984 National Football League draft.

From Bad to Worse

Following a stellar senior season, Steve was ready to begin his professional football career. The big question was which team to play for—and in what league.

The Cincinnati Bengals had the first pick in the May 1984 NFL draft and wanted Steve to play for them. But so did a new team in a new league. The United States Football League (USFL) had begun playing games during the spring of 1983. The owner of the Los Angeles Express, a team in the USFL, wanted to sign Steve, too. The Express owner offered to pay him an enormous amount of money. The complex deal would mean Steve would be paid until he was 65 years old. Steve would get $2.5 million just for signing the contract. The Express also offered to give Brigham Young University money for a scholarship in Steve's name. The Express promised Steve that he would be the starting quarterback. The Los

Angeles quarterback coach, Sid Gillman, was known as the "guru of the passing game." He could help Steve adjust quickly to the professional level.

The Cincinnati owners offered Steve a contract for less money. The Bengals told Steve they would use him as a backup quarterback, behind Ken Anderson. The Bengals wanted to work Steve into their system more slowly.

Steve struggled with his decision. After giving the matter much thought, Steve signed with the USFL team. "I don't want to look like I'm money-hungry," Steve said. "That's not what I based my decision on.

Los Angeles Express owner J. William Oldenburg, right, persuaded Steve to play for his team.

Look at my alternative in the NFL; sitting behind Ken Anderson. Who knows if I'd get a chance for three or four years."

Indeed, the money overwhelmed 22-year-old Steve. His contract was worth between $36 million and $50 million—the biggest salary in professional sports at that time. The numbers were huge, but Steve would be paid over a 43-year span. Steve's annual salary was much, much smaller than people realized. "People were calling Steve the $48 million man, (but) in reality, the value of the contract was probably between $8 million and $10 million," said Steve's agent, Leigh Steinberg. The deal paid Steve a $2.5 million signing bonus, and promised him a $2.5 million salary over four years, plus a $1.5 million loan. The remaining money would be paid to Steve in yearly checks, starting 43 years later.

When Steve got his signing bonus, he asked Steinberg to hold the check for him. "The big money really depressed Steve," Grit said. "He couldn't cope with it. He had always seen himself as a down-to-earth guy."

The USFL played its games during the spring and the Express wanted Steve to join the team in March 1984. Steve was in the middle of his last semester at Brigham Young University, and he didn't want to leave college. Grit flew out to Provo. "The money just overwhelmed him," Grit told a reporter later.

"He told me before he had to report to camp, 'I don't want to go.' I told him, 'You made a contract; you live up to the contract.'" After reminding Steve that he could finish school after the football season, Grit talked his son into joining the team immediately. Grit went with Steve to Los Angeles.

Steve's first pro game was the Express's seventh game of the season. He was so nervous, he was tongue-tied in the huddle. "He was so darned excited, he could barely call the plays," Gillman recalls. "We had to get him out and settle him down."

Gillman quickly recognized how good Steve was. Gillman told reporters that Steve was 10 levels above the rest of the league. "I said 10 years ago he was going to be one of the best quarterbacks ever," Gillman reminded people before Super Bowl XXIX. "There was nothing he couldn't do. He could run, and he could throw, and he could score."

During his first professional season, Steve became the first pro football player to rush for 100 yards and throw for 300 yards in the same game. He started 12 consecutive games. Still, his first season was difficult for him. He felt he could never live up to the expectations his enormous, well-publicized contract had created, especially since he was playing on a poor team in a weak league. "I felt in some way like my life was going down the tubes," Steve said. "You're in a crisis, and the whole world gets to watch."

Steve scrambled often while playing for the Express.

Off the field, Steve had more fun. He lived like a college student in a Redondo Beach apartment with six teammates. A multimillionaire, Steve drove around town in his old car, The Cardinal. His biggest expenses were the contributions he made, without fanfare or publicity, to his church and several charities.

In July, after the season ended, Steve went home to Connecticut for a visit. Grit put him to work—washing dishes, mowing the lawn, cleaning out the garage, and delivering newspapers on his youngest brother's paper route. In addition to working, Steve went shopping for new clothes for his family. He gave his father money to buy a Corvette that Grit had been admiring. Instead of getting the sports car, however, Grit spent the money on college tuition for Steve's brothers and sister. In the fall, Steve returned to BYU to finish his final semester. He received his bachelor's degree in international relations in December 1984.

By 1985, Steve's second pro season, the Express and the USFL were in financial trouble. The team played poorly and didn't attract many spectators. Express ticket sales were so low that the final game of the season was moved from the Los Angeles Coliseum to a small, junior college stadium 30 miles away. The players suited up and boarded the bus, but the driver refused to start the motor until he had been paid. Steve and his teammates passed a hat and collected the $500 needed to pay the driver. To no one's surprise, the USFL went out of business after the season ended.

When the USFL folded, the National Football League teams drafted the USFL players. The Tampa Bay Buccaneers had the first pick in the draft, and they chose Steve. Tampa Bay and Steve agreed to a six-year contract that would pay Steve more than $5 million. So Steve loaded up The Cardinal and drove the ancient car across the country to Florida.

Steve went to Tampa Bay after the USFL folded.

He didn't bring very impressive statistics with him to the NFL. In his two years in the USFL, Steve had passed for just 16 touchdowns. He had completed just 56 percent of his passes and he had been intercepted 22 times.

When the 1985 NFL season began that fall, Steve realized he had gone from one bad team to another. Tampa Bay's pass-protection blocking was poor, which made passing difficult for Steve. Coach Leeman Bennett designed plays in which Steve was supposed to drop back and pass. But Tampa Bay's offensive linemen weren't able to block their opponents, and Steve was often sacked.

"One time we were playing the Bears, and one of our coaches looked me right in the eye," Steve told a reporter for *Sports Illustrated.* "He said, 'Look Steve, I know everybody's kind of quit on you here. This is the kind of game where you could really get hurt. Be careful out there.' I couldn't believe it. How can you enter a game thinking like that?"

Tampa Bay's other quarterback, Steve DeBerg, tried to help Steve adjust to the NFL and to the Buccaneers. He invited Steve to his house and helped teach him the Buccaneers' offensive plays. Despite DeBerg's help, Steve and the Tampa Bay team were not suited for each other. With little or no protection, Steve began to improvise. If the receiver he wanted to throw to was covered, Steve would tuck the ball under his arm and scramble down the field.

After two seasons, Steve had passed for just 11 touchdowns. He had a 53 percent completion rate and had been intercepted 21 times. The Buccaneers won just four games during the two seasons Steve played with them.

Unhappy with the situation, Steve asked the Tampa Bay owners to trade him. His only condition, Steve said, was that he go to a team with an adequate offensive line. The Buccaneers were planning to draft University of Miami quarterback Vinny Testaverde, so they decided to honor Steve's request.

In Joe Montana's Shadow

Bill Walsh, the 49ers' head coach from 1979 through 1988, had been a fan of Steve's since he saw the quarterback play for Brigham Young University. When Coach Walsh visited the BYU campus in the spring of 1987, he watched Steve work out with his former college team. "I stood behind him (on the field) and watched him throw just about every type of pass," Walsh wrote in his book, *Building a Champion.* "I could see that he possessed a quick delivery and a fine arm."

Excited by what he saw, Walsh encouraged the 49ers to trade for Steve. On April 24, 1987, the 49ers did just that. San Francisco gave its second- and fourth-round draft picks to the Tampa Bay Buccaneers for the lefthanded quarterback.

Steve loaded up his 1976 Cadillac and drove to San Francisco. He had bought the nine-year-old car in Florida after The Cardinal, which had traveled more than a quarter of a million miles, finally broke down for good.

When Steve arrived in California, Walsh asked him to come to the 49ers' practice field for a workout. Steve was so excited that he forgot to bring his cleats. When Bronco Hinek, the 49ers equipment manager, found out that Steve wore the same size shoes as Joe Montana, he grabbed a pair out of the legendary quarterback's locker and tossed them to Steve. A longtime Montana fan, Steve didn't want to put on his hero's shoes. "Don't worry," Hinek told Steve. "Joe's not coming in today."

Thirty minutes later, Joe Montana walked in. When Coach Walsh introduced the two, Steve nervously backed up against the locker-room wall so Montana wouldn't see his jersey number, 16, written on the back of the shoes. "This was definitely not the way I envisioned meeting Joe Montana," Steve said. "I mean, this guy is a legend, and I didn't know how he'd react. Maybe he would think I was walking right in and trying to take over."

The two chatted, and Steve began to relax. Maybe he didn't notice, Steve thought. That hope was dashed, however, when Montana turned to leave. "He smiled and said 'Steve, a pleasure meeting you,'" Steve recalled. "'And, oh, by the way, nice shoes you're wearing.'"

Steve was embarrassed, but he didn't have much

time to dwell on it. Walsh and quarterbacks coach Mike Holmgren kept him busy learning the 49ers' offensive plays. Walsh gave Steve a playbook that was nearly as thick as the San Francisco phone book. When he wasn't studying the playbook, Steve was on the practice field. "We worked with him for endless hours on the fundamentals of the game, and how they applied to the 49ers offense," Walsh wrote.

When the 1987 season began, Steve spent most of his time on the bench. After all, Montana had led the 49ers to Super Bowl victories in 1982 and 1985. Steve started just one game, in mid-November, when Montana had an injured hand. Steve completed five of the six passes he threw in a 24-22 triumph over the Saints in New Orleans. He also rushed for 24 yards. A month later, Montana pulled a hamstring in the first quarter of a game at Candlestick Park against the Chicago Bears. Steve replaced him and passed for four touchdowns in a 41-0 blowout. Then he went back to the sidelines for the final two games of the regular season.

San Francisco's 13-2 record in the 1987 strike-shortened season put the 49ers in the NFC divisional playoffs against the Minnesota Vikings. San Francisco was behind 27-10 in the third quarter when Walsh sent Steve in to replace Montana. Steve outplayed Montana, scrambling for a team-high 72 yards and a touchdown. He also completed 12 of the

17 passes he attempted for 158 yards and another TD. Despite his efforts, the Vikings won, 36-24, and San Francisco's season ended. Steve headed back to his off-season home in Utah and enrolled in the Brigham Young University law school.

Coach Walsh noticed Steve's brief, but outstanding, performances. He planned to have Steve and Joe compete for the starting job in 1988. The head coach created a stir when he told reporters in the 1988 preseason that the team "may have a quarterback controversy." Although Montana was again named the starting quarterback, Walsh's comment haunted the team all year. Steve and Joe were asked regularly by reporters if there was any conflict between the two quarterbacks. Every time he was asked about Montana, Steve said that he liked and respected the older quarterback. "Joe goes out of his way to be helpful, especially when it comes to stuff outside of football," Steve told reporters.

Although he said publicly he was content with the backup role, Steve was eager to play. "Before games, Steve's bouncing off walls," teammate Randy Cross told reporters. "I've never seen enthusiasm like that." After games, if he didn't get into the contest, Steve sometimes released his energy by running up and down the sidelines. "I don't feel right about going into the clubhouse without working up a sweat," he said.

Steve and Joe Montana, right, were friends, but both wanted to play for San Francisco.

Steve did many postgame sprints in 1988. After playing in just four games, he was frustrated. "He's realistic about the situation, but that doesn't make it easier for him (to sit on the bench)," said Cross. "He can't accept it. If he ever accepted it, it wouldn't be him."

Steve made the most of every opportunity, especially his start against the Minnesota Vikings in late October. Montana was sidelined with a back injury. Steve threw a 73-yard touchdown pass to John Taylor. Then, with less than two minutes remaining in the game, and San Francisco trailing by four points, Steve dropped back to pass. When he couldn't find an open receiver, he tucked the ball under his arm and started scrambling. He dodged eight Viking defenders and sprinted 49 yards toward the end zone. With just 1 yard to go, Steve threw his body across the goal line for the game-winning touchdown in a 24-21 victory.

The 49ers finished the 1988 season with a 10-6 record and breezed through the playoffs. Steve watched from the sidelines as Joe led the team to a third Super Bowl championship. "Joe and I didn't really talk about our competition, but we didn't have to," Steve said. "We both knew the situation. Someone has to play. Someone has to sit down. I want to be on the field. I have to have that attitude. But the decision isn't mine."

The "quarterback controversy" intensified after 49ers officials talked about trading Montana to San Diego during the off-season. Newspapers and radio stations in the Bay Area ran polls asking fans who they wanted to be the 49ers quarterback. Montana was the overwhelming favorite. Back in law school, Steve paid no attention.

Bill Walsh retired as 49ers head coach in 1989. George Seifert took over the job. Although Joe was still the team's No. 1 quarterback, he had had several injuries. Steve played in 10 games and started 3.

George Seifert, right, became Steve's coach in 1989.

By that time, Steve had improved his passing. He had gotten better at finding a receiver if his first, or even second, choice was covered. He connected on 64 of 92 passing attempts that season for 1,001 yards and 8 touchdowns.

San Francisco won 14 games and returned to the Super Bowl. The 49ers blew out Denver, 55-10, in the New Orleans Superdome. Steve played briefly in the last few minutes of the game. He passed for 20 yards and scrambled for another 11 yards. Montana, the NFL's 1989 player of the year, was also the Super Bowl MVP.

Steve stayed out of the limelight, both on and off the field. Without seeking publicity, he continued to give money to his church. He also donated to youth sports programs in San Francisco and Utah, and to charities helping Navajos in four western states. He gave thousands of dollars to help a Russian family resettle in Utah. Steve also visited children in hospitals and spoke to youth groups.

Steve's playing time decreased in 1990 because Montana was healthy most of the season. Steve got into six games, completing 61.3 percent of his passes for 427 yards. In his only start, Steve rushed for 102 yards in a 13-10 loss to New Orleans.

In the final regular-season game, against Minnesota, Steve replaced Montana after halftime. The 49ers were trailing the Vikings 17-13 in the final period.

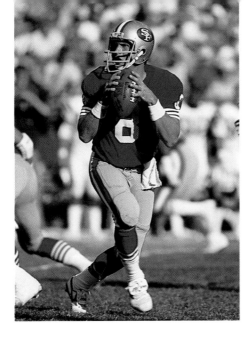

Steve led the 49ers to a thrilling victory over the Minnesota Vikings in 1990.

Then Steve connected on six of seven passes, moving the ball 88 yards. He completed the drive with a 34-yard pass to John Taylor for the game-winning TD.

The 20-17 victory raised the 49ers' record to 14-2. San Francisco's season ended three weeks later when it lost to the New York Giants, 15-13, in the NFC Championship Game.

After the season, Steve's agent urged him to ask to be traded to a team that would let him be the starting quarterback. Although Steve was frustrated by his lack of playing time, he liked living in the San Francisco area and he liked the 49ers. He decided to stick it out in San Francisco and wait for his turn. "This is the perfect system for me," Steve said. "I've put in four years waiting, and I don't want to leave just when my chance might be coming."

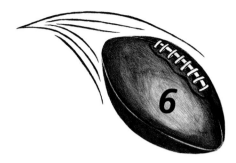

The Leader, At Last

Steve's patience was rewarded in 1991 when Coach Seifert named Steve the starting quarterback during the preseason. Montana developed tendinitis in his right elbow and had to have surgery. He would be out for the next two seasons. Meanwhile, Steve quickly established himself as one of the league's most accurate passers and fiercest competitors.

In the first game of the 1991 season, Steve threw a 73-yard touchdown pass in a 16-14 loss to the New York Giants. He completed 26 passes for 348 yards the following week and led San Francisco to a 34-14 victory over the San Diego Chargers. A month later, he set a team record when he completed 90 percent of his passes against Detroit. He connected on 18 of 20 passes for 237 yards and two touchdowns as San Francisco throttled the Lions, 35-3. A week later, the 49ers beat Philadelphia, 23-7, to even their won-lost record at 4-4.

Steve's terrific season was interrupted in November at Atlanta. A few plays after combining with John Taylor to score on a beautiful 97-yard pass play, Steve ran with the ball. He was tackled and landed awkwardly, injuring his left knee. "I got hit wrong," said Steve, who missed the next five games. Steve Bono, the third-string quarterback, replaced him.

Steve returned for the last two games of the 1991 season. In the final regular-season game, he threw for three touchdowns as the 49ers beat the Chicago Bears, 52-14. Despite missing five games in 1991, Steve led the NFL with a 101.8 quarterback rating. The quarterback rating is based on passing attempts, completions, passing yards gained, completion percentages, interceptions, and touchdowns. Quarterback ratings of 100 or more are considered excellent. Only 13 NFL quarterbacks have ever had ratings of 100 or more.

San Francisco finished with a 10-6 record, however, and failed to reach the playoffs for the first time since 1982. Disappointed fans blamed Steve. Montana's faithful supporters said that he would have gotten the team into the postseason playoffs. Steve ignored the complaints and kept quiet when he was off the playing field. The fans were emotional, Steve said. After all, Joe had led the team to four Super Bowl wins. "All this stuff, it's not negative to me," he added.

Steve is not afraid to run with the ball himself.

Back on the field in 1992, Steve became a master at reading defenses. He could adjust his offense as the play developed. If none of his receivers were open, he would throw the ball out-of-bounds. By doing that, instead of throwing near defenders or scrambling as he had in the past, Steve improved his passing. "Now I'll only run if it's a planned play or there's no other option," he said. The strategy increased his passing accuracy. In September, he passed for a career-high 449 yards against the Bills.

Jerry Rice, No. 80, and Steve have been a winning combination for San Francisco.

In October, he threw three touchdown passes to Jerry Rice as the 49ers defeated Atlanta, 56-17. In November, Steve hit Brent Jones with an 8-yard pass with 46 seconds remaining in the game, for a come-from-behind, 21-20, victory against New Orleans. A month later, Steve passed to Jerry Rice for Rice's 101st touchdown catch. That reception broke the NFL record for the most touchdown catches in a career.

As the NFL's best quarterback for the second consecutive year with a 107 quarterback rating, Steve was given many awards. *Sports Illustrated, The Sporting News*, and the NFL named Steve the Most Valuable Player in the NFL in 1992. He was the most accurate passer in the NFL with a 66.7 percent completion rate. His 25 touchdown passes also led the league. His teammates voted to give Steve the Len Eshmont award, an honor reserved for the team's most inspirational and courageous player.

Best of all, from Steve's point of view, was that the 49ers had won a league-leading 14 games (with a 14-2 record) and the NFC West Division. They had the home-field advantage in the playoffs. "If you go 14-2 and win the passing title, that's great," Steve said. "If you don't win the league championship, the title doesn't mean that much."

Steve made his first postseason start on January 9, 1993. Although Montana had returned to the team in December, Coach Seifert kept Steve as his No. 1 quarterback. In an NFC playoff game, Steve threw for two touchdowns and led San Francisco to a 20-13 victory over the Washington Redskins. After the Dallas Cowboys defeated San Francisco, 30-20, the following week in the NFC Championship Game, disappointed fans blasted Steve. They complained that he couldn't win a *big* game.

Unhappy as a backup quarterback, Montana asked the 49ers to trade him after the 1992 season. They agreed, and Montana prepared to sign an agreement with the Kansas City Chiefs. Montana's fans, however, didn't want him to go. They complained loudly and bitterly that the 49ers weren't trying hard enough to keep their hero. So in a last-ditch effort to get him to stay in San Francisco, the 49ers offered to reinstate Montana as the starting quarterback. Montana thought it over, then declined. Steve, who was studying for his final exams at BYU law school while the negotiations were taking place, shrugged it off. "Professional football's a business," Steve said. "I've put it all behind me."

With Montana gone, there was no question that Steve was the 49ers' leader. The team rallied behind him. Opponents also respected his ability. "On Sunday morning, when you have to play Steve Young, you wake up with a sickening feeling and a headache," said Tim Green, an Atlanta defensive end.

Steve's ability to read defenses thwarts opponents.

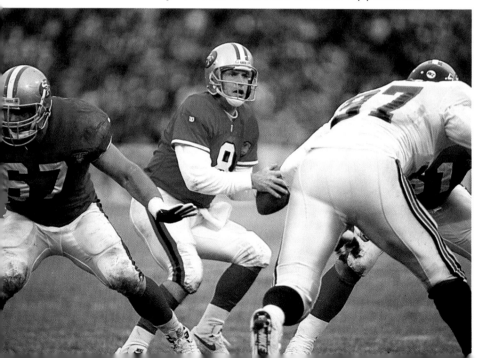

"I can honestly say those are the only times I've ever approached a game conceding that an opposing player's going to make big plays no matter what we do."

Steve passed for 29 touchdowns in 1993 and won his third straight passing title. With a 101.5 quarterback rating, Steve was the only NFL player to top a 100 rating for three years in a row. He passed for 4,023 yards, a 49ers record, and tied a team record by throwing 183 passes without an interception. Sometimes, when the 49ers were well ahead of their opponent, Coach Seifert would take Steve out and let a backup quarterback play. Steve, knowing his parents were watching the game on television, would call them from a portable telephone on the sidelines.

Steve led the 49ers to a 10-6 record and a rematch with the Dallas Cowboys in the NFC Championship Game. San Francisco lost again, 38-21. The Cowboys went on to win their second consecutive Super Bowl title. After the season ended, the 49ers and Steve agreed on a five-year contract that would pay Steve more than $26 million. He celebrated by buying his first new car, a Jeep Cherokee.

Steve was once again the most accurate passer in the league in 1994. "He's at the top of his game," Coach Seifert said. "I've never seen him play any better than this." Steve passed for 3,969 yards and 36 touchdowns and led the 49ers to a league-leading

13-3 record. Of the 461 passes he attempted, Steve completed 324, or 70.3 percent. His quarterback rating was 112.8, the highest in NFL history. He was named the league's Most Valuable Player for the second time in three seasons, and his teammates honored him with another Len Eshmont award. "We couldn't function without Steve Young," said 49ers cornerback Deion Sanders. "He is everything to this team."

Steve's leadership was instrumental to the 49ers' success in 1994. "More than anything, Steve has taken over the team as a leader, and it's really shown this year," said backup quarterback Elvis Grbac. "The confidence level he's had probably is the highest he's ever been at. He goes into a game knowing he can score points on any team."

The 49ers steamrolled the Bears in the playoffs, defeating Chicago, 44-15. For the third straight time, San Francisco faced the Dallas Cowboys for the division championship. This time the 49ers beat the Cowboys, 38-20, to get into the Super Bowl. Two weeks later, the 49ers blasted the Chargers, 49-26, for the world championship.

As the most valuable player in Super Bowl XXIX, Steve earned the respect and admiration of football fans across the country. Representatives from many different companies began calling Steve and his agent, Leigh Steinberg, as soon as the game ended.

Football fans were eager to hear what Steve had to say about winning the Super Bowl.

They all wanted Steve to appear in commercials and advertisements endorsing their products. They wanted Steve because of his exploits on the football field, as well as his honorable lifestyle. Steve donates money, without fanfare, to many charities. He created an organization, The Forever Young Foundation, to help youngsters in Utah and Northern California. "He's someone who cares a lot about the community and is enthusiastic about it," Steinberg said. "He's a true role model, a true gentleman."

Steve studied all the offers before making any decisions. He didn't want to use his name to endorse any product that he wouldn't use himself. He quickly turned down offers from tobacco companies, beer manufacturers, and even companies that produced caffeinated drinks. Using such products would conflict with Steve's Mormon beliefs. "As successful athletes go, this quarterback lives clean and is not driven by ego," Steinberg told reporters. "Consequently, he's not prone to attach his name to just anything."

Friends also say that all the attention hasn't changed Steve. When he played in the 1995 Pro Bowl, football's postseason all-star game, Steve gave tickets to several longtime friends, including Terry Lowe, his former high school math teacher. "He's still the same wonderful, humble, down-to-earth, sensitive kind of guy," said Lowe. At an NFL dinner after the Pro Bowl, Steve was surrounded by people seeking autographs, according to Lowe. "He couldn't get a bite to eat," Lowe said, "but Steve wouldn't turn anyone away." The superstar quarterback finally got a chance to eat only after security guards asked people to leave him alone.

After the Pro Bowl, Steve took a vacation to go skiing. Then he returned to his off-season home in Provo, Utah, and went back to work. Along with preparing for the 1995 football season, Steve hit the law books. After six years of attending classes during the off-season, Steve had been awarded a law degree from Brigham Young University in 1994. His next step was the bar exam, which he needed to pass before he could practice law. His goal when entering law school was to provide legal aid to people who can't afford to hire a lawyer. When his football career is over, Steve plans to become a trial lawyer. For someone like Steve, working hard and going the distance is a way of life. No matter what obstacles get in his way, he'll always come out a winner.

Steve is happy to sign autographs for his young fans, even when he's trying to eat a cookie!

CAREER HIGHLIGHTS

While playing for Brigham Young University, 1981–1983

—Named to the All-America team in 1983; runner-up for the 1983 Heisman Trophy.
—Completed 306 of 429 passing attempts for 3,902 yards and 33 touchdowns during his senior year. That was the highest single-season completion percentage in NCAA history at that time.
—Led BYU to an 11–1 season in 1983 and a Holiday Bowl victory over Missouri.
—Finished his college career with 1,084 yards rushing, 7,733 yards passing, and 72 touchdowns scored.

While playing for the Los Angeles Express, 1984–85

—Chosen in the first round of the United States Football League draft in 1984.
—Became the first pro player to rush for 100 yards and throw for 300 yards in the same game.
—Completed 56 percent of his passes during the 1984 and 1985 seasons.

While playing for the Tampa Bay Buccaneers, 1985–86

—Chosen with the first pick of the National Football League supplemental draft in 1985.
—Threw for 935 yards and 3 touchdowns in 5 games during the 1985 season.
—Completed 195 passes for 2,282 yards and 8 touchdowns during 14 games in 1986.

While playing for the San Francisco 49ers, 1987-1994

—Named Most Valuable Player of 1995 Super Bowl
—Chosen to play in Pro Bowl in 1993, 1994, and 1995.
—Regular-season statistics with the 49ers:

Season	Games Played	Passes Attempted	Passes Completed	Passing Yards	Passing TDs	Passes Intercepted	Rushes Attempted	Rushing Yards	Rushing TDs
1987	8	69	37	570	10	0	26	190	1
1988	11	101	54	680	3	3	27	184	1
1989	10	92	64	1,001	8	3	38	126	2
1990	6	62	38	427	2	0	15	159	0
1991	11	279	180	2,517	17	8	65	415	4
1992	16	402	268	3,465	25	7	75	537	4
1993	16	462	314	4,023	29	16	69	407	2
1994	16	461	324	3,969	35	10	58	293	7
1995	11	447	299	3,200	20	11	50	250	3
Total	105	2,375	1,578	19,852	149	58	423	2,561	24

ACKNOWLEDGMENTS

Photographs are reproduced with the permission of: pp. 1; 2, 6, 9, 11, 12, 61, Rob Tringali Jr./SportsChrome East/West; pp. 14, 19, Greenwich Time Photo; p. 16, Church Archives, The Church of Jesus Christ of Latter-day Saints; pp. 22, 37, AP/Wide World Photos; pp. 24, 31, 42, 47, 49, 51, 56, © Mickey Pfleger; p. 28 (both), Brigham Young University; pp. 32, 39, SportsChrome East/West; pp. 34, 40, UPI/Bettmann; pp. 52, 55, 58, © Shmuel Thaler; p. 63, BYU/Mark Philbrick.

Front cover photograph by © Mickey Pfleger. Back cover photograph by Rob Tringali Jr./Sportschrome East/West.